P9-DYE-565

cool collectibles

MILITARY COLLECTIBLES

Patrick Newell

Children's Press
A Division of Grolier Publishing
New York / London / Hong Kong / Sydney
Danbury, Connecticut

Book Design: Lisa Quattlebaum
Contributing Editor: Mark Beyer

Photo Credits: pp. 5, 27 © David Doody/FPG International; pp. 7, 40 © Photoworld/ FPG International; pp. 9, 10, 11, 17 by Laz Burke; p. 14 © John Bechtold/International Stock; p. 18 © Yogi, Inc. /Corbis; pp. 21, 26 © Archive Photos; p. 24 © Catherine Karnow/Corbis; p. 29 © Philip Gould/Corbis; p. 31 © Tony Vaccaro/Archive Photos; p. 32 © C. Lee Foster/FPG International; p. 35 © Anthony Potter Collection/Archive Photos; p. 37 © D. Wells/The Image Works.

Visit Children's Press on the Internet at:
http://publishing.grolier.com

Library of Congress Cataloging-in-Publication Data

Newell, Patrick.
Military collectibles / by Patrick Newell.
p. cm.—(Cool collectibles)
Summary: Provides an overview of the kinds of military items that are collectible, with information on value and cost, as well as help with starting a collection.
ISBN 0-516-23331-9 (lib. bdg.)—ISBN 0-516-23531-1 (pbk.)
1. Military paraphernalia—Collectors and collecting—Juvenile literature. [1. Military paraphernalia—Collectors and collecting.] I. Title. II. Series.

U790.N48 2000
355'.0075—dc21

99-058093

Printed in the United States of America
1 2 3 4 5 6 7 8 9 10 R 05 04 03 02 01 00

Contents

1	Introduction	04
2	Jimmy's Story	06
3	What's Collectible?	15
4	Value and Cost	28
	Starting Your Collection	33
	New Words	44
	For Further Reading	45
	Resources	46
	Index	47

Introduction

When you studied the American Civil War (1861–1865) in history class, did you ever wonder what it was like to be there? What kinds of clothes did they wear and how did they look? Were their muskets heavy? Were their bayonets sharp? Some people know the answers to these questions. Many of these people collect military weapons and gear. These collectibles are called militaria.

Militaria include uniforms, equipment, medals, firearms, blades, patches, and vehicles. These collectibles can come from all countries and any time throughout history. There is a huge amount of militaria available for collectors throughout the world. Anyone at any age has a chance to begin collecting.

People begin collecting militaria for different

Military collectibles can come from different wars and different eras. This photo shows people using real muskets to stage a past American Civil War battle.

reasons. Some people collect for an object's artistic value. Others collect for historical value. A third type of collector collects for investment value. Once interested, collecting often lasts a lifetime.

1

Jimmy's Story

Jimmy set up his small table in the cafeteria of the Special Training and Army Review Unit. He placed his newspapers on top of this table. Beside the newspapers was an old cigar box to collect the money he earned from selling papers. Jimmy lived in Lincoln, Nebraska. The year was 1943. Lincoln was a central stopover for soldiers returning from World War II. This barracks was used for men who were being moved to different units. It was also used for special training. Jimmy knew that there were a lot of men living at the barracks. He knew that they all wanted newspapers to learn what was happening in the war.

Because the soldiers were being switched to different units, they no longer needed their current unit patches. These patches were colorful

This collection of World War I badges shows the many different styles used by units fighting in the war.

M
TANK
80 DIV
91
WW
AA
5
28
93
37
29
83
79
90 div.

and showed what each unit did. The patches from tank units had tank treads and cannons on them. The patches that the flyers wore were blue and had shooting stars and wings. Jimmy asked every soldier who bought a newspaper from him if he could have that soldier's unit patch. Most of the soldiers gave him their patches. The servicemen all liked Jimmy because he was friendly. They liked buying papers from him.

Sometimes, Jimmy would see a patch that he wanted but did not have yet. Jimmy would ask the man if he could have the patch. Sometimes just asking got him the patch. If he had to, Jimmy would offer a free newspaper to the soldier in trade for the patch. Jimmy wanted to get as many patches as he could. He wanted to collect all the unit patches from all of the different American units that fought in World War II (1939–1945).

Jimmy didn't get them all. However, he did collect more than one hundred patches of all

U.S. Army 101st
Airborne Division
patch from WWII

different colors and shapes. He sewed the patches onto a large blanket. He hung the blanket from the wall to show the patches off to his friends.

Jimmy had three favorite patches. One patch was black and had a bald eagle on it. This patch was from the 101st Airborne Division. This division fought in the invasion of Normandy. Another of his favorites was a

1st Cavalry patch

patch from the 1st Cavalry. The 1st Cavalry fought in the Philippines. Their patch was yellow with a horse's head on it. Jimmy's third favorite patch was from the 1st Infantry. This Infantry was known as the "Big Red One." They fought in the Battle of the Bulge near the end of the war. Their patch was square and green. It had a red number "1" in the middle. Jim still has this patch collection today. He enjoys showing it to people.

U.S. Army 1st Infantry patch

Patch collecting is only one way to become involved in collecting militaria. It is inexpensive and fun. The patches are colorful, and each one means something.

A patch from the 1st Cavalry has the entire history of that unit behind it. They fought against the Native Americans at the end of the last century. They also fought in World War II. They gave up their horses for helicopters and were one of the most famous fighting units in the Vietnam conflict.

There are other ways to explore military history. There are many things that people collect, such as awards, uniforms, weapons and equipment, and even vehicles.

The cavalry used to be made up of horses. Today the U.S. Army's cavalry are helicopter units. These units have patches that identify them.

AIRBORNE
2
AMERICAN CAMPAIGN
DEUTSCHLAND
Internationaler Kraftfahrzeugverkehr
Internationaler Führerschein
Internationales Abkommen vom 24. April 1926
Ausstellung
Ort:
Tag:
Dienst-Stempel
Landratsamt
(Unterschrift)
Behörden- und Industrie-Verlag GmbH, Frankfurt a. M.

2

What's Collectible?

Anything having to do with the military is collectible. From bullets to zippered parkas, collectors have thousands of objects from which to choose. You can collect objects from the most recent war, or from any war throughout history. Only your desire and imagination are needed to begin collecting. There are five kinds of military collectibles most popular today. They are medals, uniforms, helmets and headdress, insignia and badges, and weapons.

MEDALS

A medal is given to a soldier for something he or she has done. Medals are given for bravery,

Some of the most popular World War II collectibles include medals, helmets, and weapons.

fighting in a battle, or for the number of years a soldier spent in the military. A medal has a hanging metal ornament attached to a ribbon. This metal ornament is called a pendant.

Collecting medals is a great way to learn about history. As you collect, you should learn something about the wars from which you have collected objects. By reading about the history of a war, you may learn a lot about the collectibles. Take medals, for instance. Would you know the difference between a World War I (1914–1918) medal and a medal from the American Civil War? If you read about the history of both those wars, you may find many pictures of medals given to the soldiers who fought in those wars.The most prized medal is one that comes with some written paperwork. The paperwork may be a letter of thanks often given with medals to a soldier. These letters have the name of the person who received the medal and the person who awarded the medal. Letters

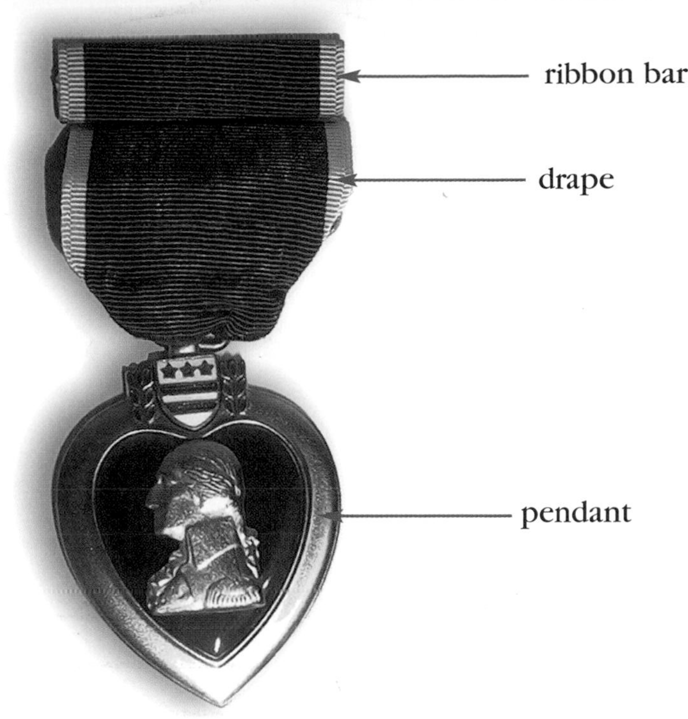

There are three parts to each medal: the ribbon bar, the drape, and the pendant. This is a Purple Heart, awarded to a soldier who has been wounded in battle.

may also say what the soldier did to deserve the medal. The story that gives the history of the medal is important to collectors. For example, one collector has a group of World War II Distinguished Flying Cross medals. These medals were given for bravery and success while flying an airplane. Besides the importance of the medals, this collection has historical arti-

This photo shows the ribbons of a submarine officer's dress uniform. Each ribbon shows a different military campaign, or award from a foreign country. Ribbons can even show a soldier's rank.

facts that came with it. These artifacts include the pilot's flying logbook, pictures of the pilot with his British Halifax bomber, and original military service documents. With this information, the collector can find out a great deal about the pilot. The collector can learn about the pilot's family, his unit, and maybe about what happened to him after the war.

Medals are also designed to be beautiful. They are artistic. One medal has several different parts. Knowing these parts and their purpose is important when collecting. The medal itself is called the pendant. The colorful ribbon that holds the medal is called the drape. The ribbon bar is at the top, and is used to pin the medal to a uniform. The ribbon bar is worn without the medal or ribbon attached to it when a soldier is not in uniform. Ribbon bars are the colorful strips that you often see above the left breast pocket on soldiers' uniforms. The color of the drape and the design of the pendant identify the medals.

UNIFORMS

Soldiers have been wearing uniforms since 1660. This was just after the British Civil War (1642–1651). Before then, soldiers wore real oak leaves or different colored flowers to tell who was on which side. Since that time uniforms have been an important part of being a soldier. Soldiers have several uniforms for different events. A dress uniform is a uniform used only for special times, such as for ceremonies. Battledress is the outfit used while fighting the enemy. Since the dress uniform is not used as often, many still exist for collectors to buy. However, dress uniforms are not as collectible as battledress uniforms. This is because collectors want uniforms that were actually worn by soldiers during battle. Therefore, the battledress an officer wore at the Battle of the Bulge (1944) in World War II would be more collectible than the dress uniform that hung in his closet on the same day. The value of a ripped, stained, and muddy uniform also depends on knowing who wore it, and in what battle. This is another reason you should learn something about war history. Knowing where troops fought and during what battles will help you to be a better collector. Today, collectors want uniforms from Nazi Germany and those having anything to do with an Airborne or Paratrooper division.

HEADDRESS

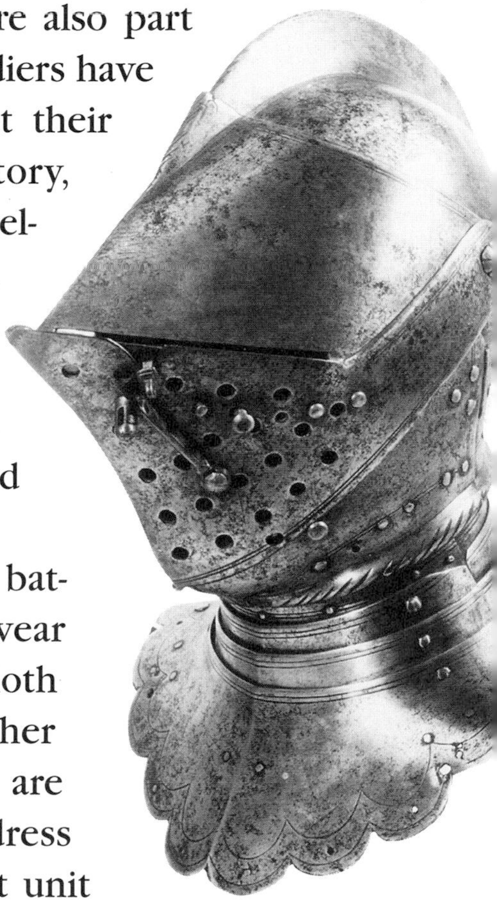

Helmets and headdress are also part of a soldier's uniform. Soldiers have always needed to protect their heads. Throughout history, many different styles of helmets have been invented. Medieval (500–1500) knights wore polished steel helmets that covered the entire head and neck.

When away from the battlefield, soldiers didn't wear helmets. They wore a cloth cap with a patch or other insignia attached. These are called headdress. Headdress showed to which combat unit

16th Century French helmet used as armor.

the soldier belonged. Through the years these leather or cloth caps and hats have been made in many different styles.

Helmets and headdress are very popular today for three reasons. First, the many styles from different countries look cool. Second, many are still in excellent condition because helmets were made to last. Finally, many millions were made for the fighting soldiers. This means that thousands of both used and new helmets are available to collectors. The most popular helmets today are the M1916 German steel helmet from World War II, and the U.S. Airborne or Paratrooper helmets.

INSIGNIA AND BADGES

Each fighting unit wore specially designed badges or insignia to separate them from other units. Badges are bits of metal, brass, or polished aluminum with different designs that show the unit or rank. One example from World War II is a set of wound badges, made of gold, silver, and bronze, presented by Adolf Hitler. Each shows crossed swords in the background, with a German helmet in the foreground. These were given to soldiers who were wounded in combat. A set like this is expensive for the beginning collector. However, there are other badges to be found that cost much less. Look for basic rank badges (Private or Corporal) and insignia pins.

Insignia are usually cloth patches or designs sewn on to the uniform. The U.S. military uses cloth patches today, but it was not always so. During World War I the 81st Division wore a design on their uniform in the shape of a wildcat. General Pershing, the commander of U.S. troops, ordered the design removed. He wanted everyone to look alike. However, Pershing found that troop spirit fell after his decision. He gave the 81st back their Wildcat. He also allowed other divisions to make their own designs. Today, each unit has its own colorful patch.

In the United States and Canada, unit patch collecting is easy and inexpensive. Remember Jimmy's newspaper stand? There is a huge selection from each country's military units, past and present, from which to choose. As Jimmy found out, each patch carries the history of that unit with it. One fun part of collecting is finding a unit design that is rare and hard to find. These rare patches can cost a lot of money. However, they don't cost as much as uniforms or helmets.

One such patch is a red arrowhead with the letters "USA" written across the top and the letters CANADA written down its length. This was the patch for the 1st Special Service Force. This unit carried out duties behind enemy lines. Both American and Canadian troops wore this patch, making it unique.

Unit patches often tell a collector what that unit does.

WEAPONS

Collectors are interested in all types of weapons used in battle. Crossbows, swords, knives, spears, axes, pistols, rifles, muskets, bayonets, and even bombs all are collectible. Most antique guns and rifles have their firing pins removed for safety. Some of these weapons can be expensive for a beginning collector. Also, to collect large blades and firearms, you must be of a certain age. Some weapons may even be illegal to own. These laws are different depending on where you live. You should learn these laws before you begin collecting.

Bayonets (long knives attached to the end of a rifle or musket) are the least expensive of the edged weapons. Plus, they are easier to find. Unlike swords, which were carried by officers, common soldiers used bayonets.

Swords are a special part of military collectibles. They are usually well-crafted and beautiful weapons. Because officers used swords

Swords are important symbols of war. Remember King Arthur's legendary sword, Excalibur? There are many stories of swords and famous sword fighters in history. Today, you can find pictures of swords on the military patches, medals, and insignia of almost every country in the world.

in battle, the history of the sword is easier to find out about. Also, swords can be very valuable because of the skill with which they were made and the history behind many of them.

Firearms come in many different types and sizes. There are antique pistols, rifles, handguns, muskets, and machine guns. Also, many collectible firearms are easy to find because so many hundreds of thousands were made and given to soldiers. Some types of guns and rifles are more popu-

Common soldiers used bayonets. Bayonets are easier to find as a collector and they cost less.

lar collectibles than others. Look for the Colt Naval revolver of 1851, and the "Brown Bess" musket (used by British soldiers for almost a hundred years from the 17th and 18th centuries). You can also find the more modern semiautomatic guns of World War II, such as the U.S. Army Officer Colt .45 or the German Luger.

3

Value and Cost

It's important that every collector know something about how much collectibles cost. A couple of simple questions can be helpful when shopping for military collectibles. Is the price fair? Is the item real or a fake? Unlike most items, you can't return a military collectible once you've bought it. However, the more important question remains: What is the value to you?

WEAPONS AS ART

Officers in all countries have carried swords. Because officers had money, their weapons were often made by hand. Handmade swords are beautiful weapons. Sabers carried by officers in the American Civil War are a good example.

This American Civil War officer's dress sword and leather gauntlet make it easy to see why some weapons are considered art.

A Rich Presentation Sword used by a Union officer had carvings of goddesses in the handle and came with a silver scabbard (holder). There were lion's heads in the guard (the part that protects the hand).

AN INVESTMENT IN ARTIFACTS

Collecting militaria is definitely an investment. Collectors buy an object and then may choose to keep it for many years. They will wait for the price to increase in order to sell it at a profit. Many collectors do not have a lot of money. Yet they still would like to have nice objects to display. They may also want to learn about history, or keep the memory of a soldier alive. There are many ways to do these things without spending a lot of money.

Collectors who collect for value are willing to pay more for rare items. They are willing to pay more for items for many reasons. Maybe the object has an interesting historical background.

Helmets, uniforms, weapons, and ammunition are all artifacts of past wars which are collectible.

Maybe there is proof as to who owned or used the piece. However, the high cost of some objects is not a reason to give up a desire to collect militaria. In fact, collecting modern-day military items can be a wise investment. Think about buying Gulf War military collectibles. Right now many of those items are inexpensive. However, in a few years they may rise in value.

4

Starting Your Collection

You can learn a lot more about military collectibles by reading books and magazines about the history of certain wars. Plus, you'll learn more than war history when reading books about wars. You'll also learn about the people and places of those times. If you like the uniforms that American Civil War soldiers wore, then read about that war. Learn about the people who lived in the Confederate States of America. You will be able to learn why the Union troops wore blue uniforms, and why the Confederate troops wore gray uniforms. If you like the medals and badges used by different countries during World War II, then learn more

Do you know why Union troops wore blue uniforms? By reading books about war history, you can learn about the people and places of those times.

about that war. Did you know that a world war is called a world war because most nations of the world somehow took part? You'll be able to discover which country fought during the war, and in what part of the world. You'll learn about why nations were fighting. And you'll learn why other nations—such as Switzerland—did not fight at all. The history connected to militaria is as interesting as are the collectibles themselves.

Besides reading about wars, you can also visit museums. Did you know many art museums have military items in their collections? Suits of armor, shields, axes, and many kinds of knives and swords all are considered art objects. They were made in such a way that is so beautiful, they are now collected in museums for everyone to see and admire. You might try searching the Internet to find out if the museums in your area have militaria in their collections.

Once you learn more about military col-

As soldiers were captured in battle, their helmets, flags, and weapons were taken. Now collectors have them.

lectibles and the history behind them, you must ask yourself why you want to collect. For value and investment? For historical study? For artistic delight? Many collectors collect for all of these reasons. Why do you want to collect military artifacts?

THE MILITARIA MARKETPLACE

The most popular collectible items available for sale come from three different areas: Nazi Germany, America, and Imperial Germany (before 1920). By kind, the most common collectibles are: helmets and caps, edged weapons, firearms, uniforms, and metal insignia. Keep in mind that these are the most popular, but not the only collectibles available. If you like American Civil War belt buckles, there are many for sale. How about the many different kinds of U.S. or Canadian dress hats available? If you like headdress from a certain country or war, all you need to do is search and you can find these items. In fact, much of the fun in collecting is the hunt for an item you want to have for your collection. Once you find it and are able to buy that object, you experience a great feeling of success.

WHERE TO LOOK

Flea markets are great places to begin your search for military collectibles. People often have a variety of badges, medals, and edged weapons available for sale. Be careful, though. You will want to know what you are getting for

Flea markets are a great place to start looking for military collectibles. Sometimes rare items can be found there.

your money. The most important thing you want to know is whether the item is the real thing. To know what you're looking for, you really have to do your homework.

Collectible fairs and shows often take place in the major cities of the United States and Canada. Tables and booths are set up to show off the various items for sale by dealers and other collectors.

Some people make a living by buying and selling militaria. They are known as dealers. Dealers have shops as do sporting goods or clothing stores. Dealers' prices for collectibles are higher than those you can find at flea markets or shows. They also will pay a lot less for items collectors wish to sell to them. Dealers are in the business to make a profit. To do this they must buy items at a lower price than their actual value. Then they sell them at a higher price. However, sometimes a dealer has something that you simply must have for your collection. You will have to decide how much that item is really worth to you.

CARING FOR MILITARIA

In general, common sense is important when caring for military collectibles. A collector is taking care of a piece of history. You shouldn't damage these collectibles when you store or handle them. However, all collectors want to display their collections for people to see.

Here are some rules to follow. Certain types of cloth will wear out in time if not taken care of properly. Fabrics fade when placed in direct sunlight. This means ribbons, uniforms, patches, and all other fabric items should not be placed in areas where the sun can reach them. Also, some uniforms or patches need to be washed. You should not clean uniforms or patches with the harsh soaps and detergents used for your everyday clothing. Let a professional clean them for you.

Be aware that metal can tarnish and change color. Also, metal often collects particles from the air that can ruin its finish. Some metals need oiling to keep their shine and resist damage. Metal awards and insignia should be cleaned by professionals (or not at all if bought in good condition). After cleaning they should be sealed in an airtight case for display.

Collecting militaria is a great way to learn about history and warfare. Best of all, you can meet people and make friends. Have fun and good hunting!

Ribbons, uniforms, and patches should not be stored in direct sunlight. Sunlight makes fabric colors fade.

Timeline

American Revolution (1775-1783)

The American Revolution was fought between the North American colonies and the British. The colonies opposed Britain's taxes and unjust laws. The colonists wanted political freedom, but Britain did not want to give them that freedom. The conflict became an international war when France, Spain, and the Netherlands joined forces with the American colonies. The colonists declared freedom on July 4, 1776, a day that would come to be known as Independence Day. The fighting continued until 1783.

The Civil War (1861-1865)

The Civil War started as a conflict about whether slavery should be allowed in the United States. The Northern states were against slavery. However, the Southern states' economy depended on slavery, so they opposed the antislavery efforts. In order to preserve their state rights, the Southern states split away from the rest of the country to become the Confederate States of America. The North and the South went to battle against each other. The war between the North and the South ended when the South surrendered in 1865.

World War I (1914-1918)

This international war between the Central Powers (Germany,Austria-Hungary, and Turkey) and the Allies (France, Great Britain, Russia, Italy, Japan, and the United States) began with the assassination of Francis Ferdinand, the archduke of Austria. A Serbian was blamed for the murder. Austria planned to punish Serbia. This plan caused a war between European nations. In 1918, Germany was unable to fight any longer. They signed an agreement with the Allied forces to end the war.

World War II (1939-1945)

After the Germans were defeated in World War I, Adolf Hitler rose to power. He began to rebuild the German military in preparation for another war. Germany, Italy, and Japan (the Axis Powers) fought against France, Great Britain, the United States, the Soviet Union, and China (the Allies). After a six-year battle, the Axis Powers were defeated. Hitler killed himself in March, 1945, and Germany surrendered. Japan surrendered after the bombing of Hiroshima and Nagasaki.

Vietnam War (1964-1973)

The Vietnam War was fought between communist North Vietnam and the republic of South Vietnam. South Vietnam and the United States joined forces to oppose the North Vietnamese leadership. They did not want communism to spread into the south. The United States fought this war with South Vietnam. In 1968 the American public grew tired of the war. Protests against the war forced the U.S. government to pull its troops out of Vietnam. The war ended with a communist victory and takeovers in Cambodia and Laos.

Persian Gulf War (1991)

Saddam Hussein, the leader of Iraq, wanted control of Kuwait because of their large oil fields. Dozens of nations around the world joined together to fight the Iraqis. The United States led the first attack on Iraq, hoping to force Hussein to withdraw from Kuwait. The attacks on Iraq crushed its army and it was unable to go on fighting. Iraq's dangerous weapons were destroyed and Kuwait was freed.

New Words

artifact something made by human hands, often an antique or ancient item

battledress the uniform a soldier wears in the field during combat

drape the cloth part of a medal that holds the medal

dress uniform the uniform a soldier wears for special occasions

lapel bars worn by veterans showing medals they have won during their years in service

militaria items and artifacts having to do with warfare

morale the emotional condition of a group of soldiers

novice beginner

pendant the metal portion of a medal

ribbon bar the portion of a medal that pins to the uniform and holds the drape

suspension ribbon the cloth part of a medal which holds the pendant

For Further Reading

Austin, Richard J. *Official Price Guide to Military Collectibles.* New York, House of Collectibles, 1998.

Emerson, William K. *Encyclopedia of United States Army Insignia and Uniforms.* Norman, OK: University of Oklahoma Press, 1996.

Morgan, J.L. Pete, and Ted A. Thurman. *American Military Patch Guide.* Greenville, SC: Medals of America, 1997.

Schuyler, Hartley and Graham. *Illustrated Catalog of Civil War Military Goods.* New York: Dover, 1985.

Sterne, Gary, and Irene Moore. *The International Military Collectors Guide.* New York: Arms and Armour, 1997.

Resources

Organizations and Museums

American Society of Military History
Los Angeles Patriotic Hall
1816 S. Figueroa
Los Angeles, CA 90015

National Firearms Museum
1600 Rhode Island Avenue
Washington, D.C. 20036

Web Sites

Medals of America Press
http://www.usmedals.com
This site includes many links to learn about military history. Learn the stories behind a variety of medals badges, patches, ribbons, and insignia.

The Orders and Medals Society of America
http://www.omsa.org
Learn about Orders of Chivalry, decorations, medals, and other honors given by nations around the world.

Index

A

American Civil War, 4, 16, 28, 33, 36
armor, 34
artifact, 17, 18
artistic value, 5, 34, 35
axes, 25, 34

B

badges, 15, 22, 23, 33, 36
battledress, 20
Battle of the Bulge, 11, 20
bayonets, 4, 25
blades, 4
British Civil War, 19
"brown bess" musket, 27

C

cavalry, 10, 13
Colt .45, 27

D

dealers, 38
drape, 19
dress uniform, 19, 20

F

firearms, 4, 25, 26, 36
flea markets, 36, 38

H

handgun, 26
headdress, 15, 21, 22, 36
helmet, 15, 21-24, 36
historical value, 5, 35
Hitler, Adolf, 23

I

Imperial Germany, 35
insignia, 15, 21-23, 36, 39
investment value, 5, 31

L

Luger, 27

M
medals, 4, 15–19, 33, 36
Medieval, 21
militaria, 4, 30, 31, 34, 38, 39
militaria (care of), 39
museums, 34
musket, 4, 25, 26

N
Nazi, 20, 35

P
paperwork, 16
patches, 4, 7–13, 21, 23, 24, 39
pendant, 16, 19
Pershing, General, 23
Persian Gulf War, 31
pistol, 25, 26

R
ribbon bar, 19
rifle, 25, 26

S
sabers, 28
scabbard, 29
shields, 34
swords, 23, 25, 26, 28, 34

T
tanks, 8

V
value, 28, 29, 35
vehicles, 4, 13
Vietnam War, 13

W
weapons, 13, 15, 25, 35, 36
World War I, 16, 23
World War II, 6, 8, 13, 17, 20, 22, 27, 33

About the Author

Patrick Newell has had an interst in militaria since his youth. He has a BA in English from Illinois State University, and is an active Eagle Scout. He resides in Chicago, Illinois.